How Great Thou Art, Almighty!

A sincere ode dedicated to God Almighty

Thomas Kavil

Made with ♥ on the BookLeaf Publishing Platform
www.bookleafpub.in
www.bookleafpub.com

Dedication

Being my first written work to be published; I humbly dedicate this work to the Almighty God. The title "How great thou art, Almighty!" is a constant exclamation my heart shouts whenever I try to comprehend the ways of God showing mercy to His creation. Since there is nothing that the humankind, the creation can offer to the creator, but only what has been given as talents, knowledge and skill by God Himself; I consider my writing as one of God's gifts to me. Despite of many imperfections in this book, despite of not being a polished, experienced and professional writer, I would dedicate my first published work to Him; because I know He considers the intention rather than looking for perfection.

Preface

Just an ordinary kid who have never written any piece of writing at professional level, but have always enjoyed using words to express feelings, thoughts and experiences; both personal and observed. One day, he thought of praising God through the small set of words he has got in his vocabulary. I would not consider myself a poet, but I still tried writing poetry from a Christian perspective, based on my experiences, with an intention of making the readers connect with the words I used, with their personal feelings and consider this their own ode to the Lord Almighty.

Acknowledgements

I express my gratitude to the Lord Almighty for blessing me with the skill to join the words and presenting it to the readers.

I am thankful to my family and dear friends who appreciated and encouraged my little hobby of writing.

A special thanks to the BookLeaf Publishing Company for their encouraging #21dayswritingchallenge which made me consider to write something with an intention to get it published.

Also thanking all the readers who made a choice to read this book.

1. Your Wonderful Creation

When I see all the things You created, all things alive and
breathing,
I amaze at the portion of love You poured into each
being.
Amidst the chaos within me, I find seeing Your
wonderful creation soothing,
Even if the world doesn't value me, I know in Your court
I'm seen.

You put the glorious clouds in the skies you painted with
shades of blue,
Placed the moon, embedded many stars and fixed the
sun shining so bright.
The earth you decorated with the flowers of different
hue,
The greens and yellows, the reds and pinks; all lovely to
the sight.

You made the ground and assigned place for the seas,
Created the beasts of the land and the fishes of the

ocean.
From the ground bloomed the flowers and they attracted
the bees,
At Your voice even the unseen winds came to motion.

To the calm nature, You also gave a violent side,
I wonder if that's all a reflection of your love turning
into a displeasure.
The majestic dimensions of this universe only You could
decide,
The limits of the high sky and the deep ocean only You
can measure.

All glory to You for this mighty works of Your hand,
Everything in existence will be grateful because You
have treasured us in Your heart.
For the grace You offered, with awe in Your assembly we
will stand,
With no other words in our mouths, but our tongues
only praising, "How great thou art!"

2. My Creator

You have known me even before I was conceived in my
mother's womb,
You chose to bring me into existence and have numbered
my days till I sleep in my tomb.
You put so much thought in weaving every part of me so
intricately,
You are so powerful, yet you dealt with me so delicately.
You gave me the power to make choices every day,
You observed every decision I took, every step I put on
my way.
You knew I'll make the wrong choices, on my path I'll
stumble,
You still had nothing but only mercy which did not let
me crumble.
You made me a masterpiece, just like the clay taking
form in the hands of a potter,
You never left me, even when I strayed away from my
creator.
You gave me life, without you I have no worth,
You had thought of me even before my birth.

You are my God, I know even my death couldn't do us
part,
You created me so wonderfully, Oh Lord how great thou
art!

3. My Fall

How I stumbled, How I fell!
Oh God! The state of my misery only I can tell.
I let myself fall deep into the dark zone,
I thought it'd be fun, but ultimately I found myself alone.
Embarrassed with myself, I thought of returning back,
Hoping if You accept me even as your servant, I will
never lack.
I was too confident to go away from You into this
attractive place,
Little did I know then, that I was drifting away from
Your grace.
I had everything, still from within I felt hollow,
I was chasing the world; and You, I failed to follow.
But I know how great thou art! In You I will believe,
In Your mercy; not as a servant but as Your child I will
live.
How I stumbled, How I fell!
Oh God! This time it was at Your feet, so everything is
well.

4. Who is my God?

Once a dear acquaintance asked me, "Who is your God?"
The question seemed so simple, I was sure to have an
answer;
But I wondered if I could describe my God the way I see
Him,
This made my heart heavy and I asked myself, "Who is
my God?"

I closed my eyes, tried to find peace in my chaotic mind,
I searched within myself, my God I tried to find.
In that moment, everything was silent, everything got
still,
I remembered the great love, the ultimate sacrifice made
on that hill.

The question was answered, the burden on my heart was
taken,
In that answer I remembered my God's love, that I was
not forsaken.
I went to describe my friend about the one I worship, the

one I praise,
To tell that a sinner like me has a chance to live, only
because of His grace.

My God is the creator of the heavens and earth, of things
seen and unseen,
He is the artist of the masterpiece called life, the best of
all arts that have ever been.
Made me in His own image, loved me as His own child,
Taking care of me in my paths, my light and my guide.

The One with the authority over most violent sea and the
most ferocious wild beast,
He blessed His people in the wilderness by offering them
the heavenly feast.
In His mercy, chose to be limited in human form;
humbling Himself to death,
For His love I will praise, "How great thou art!" with my
every breath.

But that's not all, He rose again; even over death His
command was declared,
He showed that He is not just a King but also a loving
father who cared.
To my friend who asked me about my God; this is what I
said;
The price of the sins I committed, in His love, He paid.

5. Teach me Your ways

Teach me Your ways, God;
Teach me how to have faith that pleases You.
I have heard and known about Your wonders,
I am aware, beyond my imaginations are Your powers.
Teach me to walk on righteous ways, to look beyond evil distractions;
Teach me to resist the temptations, to submit my faith even through my actions.
I want to glorify You in my grief,
I want to praise You in my pain,
I want to delight in You through the disasters,
I want to trust in You during troubles,
I want to surrender to You in my sadness,
I want to hope in You in my helplessness.
Even in my worst I only need You and acknowledge You in my best,
Let me lean on no one and nothing else; may only in You I find my rest.
Teach me how to have faith that moves mountains, the faith that doesn't keep us apart;

Teach me how to praise You through my life; my God,
how great thou art!
Teach me how to love like You, how to forgive like You;
Teach me Your ways my God, I want to be like You.

6. Omniscient

In this world, I am surrounded by darkness and my soul
is weak,
I can trust no man because their selfish glory do they
seek.
Despite of being surrounded by the people who claim to
love me,
The state I eventually find myself is full of despair and
lonely.

How can I blame the world, even I get distracted, I feel
lost;
When people try to seek my help, I end up favoring
them with a cost.
The ones You created, have made their choice and it is
wrong,
Worldly pleasures feel good for a moment but they don't
last long.

In Your mercy, You are still waiting for us to return,
It is Your patience, You are letting us learn.

Even if we go astray, we know you will be there,
Like a shepherd keeping an eye on His sheep out of His
care.

I can never run so far and hide from Your sight,
No darkness can cover me which can't be removed by
Your light.
Keep me close to You, guide me to walk only on
righteous ways,
How great thou art Almighty, Your praises I'll sing
always.

7. Strength in Your presence

There are times when I look around and find myself
alone,
I realize the decisions I made, the choices I selected were
wrong.
Blinded by this world and all that it had to offer, far from
You, I was gone;
So many promises of forever with people, but I
understood in the journey of life, stays no one.

I stumbled in my life, lost my strength along the way,
My eyes try searching for someone who can lift me up,
who would stay.
Thought I was still near You, but found myself very far
away,
Afraid of the darkness, I keep waiting for the sunshine,
to see the bright day.

Then I remembered, though I went astray, Your eyes
were always there,
I am imperfect, I may forget; but like a loving mother,

You would still care.
With You on my side, all troubles and pain I can bear,
My adversary cannot destroy me; they know You are my
protector, they wouldn't dare.

How great thou art, Almighty! I find my strength in Your
presence,
You hear my cry from afar, from distance my fear You
can sense.
How can I describe Your greatness, there exists no
worthy word or sentence,
I will dedicate my life to You, in Your court this sinner
will kneel in repentance.

The sevenfold blazing furnace cannot burn me, You are
the fourth man in there to save me;
I can be surrounded by the hungry lions, but to satisfy
their hunger they couldn't have me.
You tell me a stone and the sling is enough, because You
are bigger than the giant I can see;
I need not fear the storm, as You have command even
over the mighty waves of sea.

8. Jehovah Nacham

Afraid of the darkness, when I sit alone and weep,
All the nights where I would cry myself to sleep,
I wonder if there is anyone who would understand, who
would care;
Is life the same for everyone or just for me, is it unfair?

Then would I realize, coming back to my sense,
Sin is on me, I went away from Your presence.
Everyday I woke up was a new chance for me,
Each day got wasted in distraction instead of looking
upon Thee.

Still I know You are quick to forgive and slow to anger,
Your mighty arms would shield me against every danger.
I may fall due to my folly, but You won't let me get
destroyed,
For I worship the living God, my prayers don't go into a
void.

You are merciful to wipe away my tears,

Staying by my side, letting me face all my fears.
Out of Your love, You choose to keep me close to Your
heart,
Despite of my sins You welcome me; Oh how great thou
art!

No darkness shall overpower me, for Your light shines
brighter,
You would protect me under Your mighty wings, Jehovah
Nacham, my comforter.
Life might not be same for everyone, not even fair to all,
But there's the One who cares, run to Him and we would
never fall.

9. Compassionate King

According to Your will we came into existence,
You have decided every breath we have till we eternally
sleep.
No matter how far we try to run or how hard we try to
hide,
We cannot run away from Your glorious presence.

This is Your world, everything lives by Your order,
You are the King of kings, everything is under Your
power.
Despite of having the authority to destroy us, You
choose to forgive,
Such great is Your mercy, Your love cannot be bound by
any border.

You have an account of every tear that roll down from
our eyes,
Our struggles and sufferings did not go unnoticed by
Your sight.
Difficult times were a consequence of our bad choice,

Still You decided to lift us up and answer our cries.

Oh King at Your command even the mountains move
and the seas roar,
Yet You considered us worthy enough to give us the gift
of free choice.
We got distracted, took the wrong options, always
hurting You,
Worst things were supposed to be in our cup, but the
weight of our sins You bore.

This is Your compassion, the love for Your creation,
Withholding the punishment we deserve and offering
the mercy we are unworthy of.
How great thou art Almighty! You are worthy of all the
praise,
We are not perfect, but if it Your will, we know through
You we will receive salvation.

10. The Good Shepherd

I am one of the sheep in Your precious herd,
Silly, distracted and a whole lot of coward.
Straying away always, causing You to worry,
Always ending up in a mess for You to clean, I am sorry.
You have taught me to look for the traps, warned me
about the enemy's snare,
Given me knowledge to keep away from the illusions
and to be always aware.
Yet my mind gets lured by the glittering decoy and I end
up chasing the bait,
Eventually I fall into the trap, hurting and full of filth; in
desperation, for You I wait.
Out of love, You leave the ninety nine and come looking
for the silly me,
I couldn't comprehend how could You love me so much,
what worth in me do You see.
You take me out of the messy pit and clean me, making
me pure again,
How great thou art! Only You can wipe away my every
stain.

Out of all the sheep, I am the most foolish one of the
herd,
You still choose to rescue me; indeed You are the good
shepherd.

11. Surrender

I might have planned big things for myself, but only
Yours would prevail,
The confidence I build of having figured everything
alone would fail.
In everything I do, I would need You to be my guide,
Even all good things would end up in vain if You are not
by my side.

When everything feels overwhelming, when all doors
seems shut,
Even when I am not sure where to look, in You alone
would I trust.
I know things were never in my control, but You have
the authority over all,
In my foolishness, I may have to stumble, but I believe
You will not let me fall.

Every step I take, in every decision I make, You will be
my counsellor,
I will not walk in evil ways; righteous paths will I

choose, if to You I surrender.
Evil may look at me and wonder, trying new methods to
trap and deceive,
But every time evil would fail as God has a hold on me,
my hands He would never leave.

How great thou art Almighty! Nothing can separate
what You have brought together,
Even if humans think we have the best plans, You would
always have something better.
Surrendering to You despite of not understanding Your
ways is the wisest choice anyone could make,
We know You have the best in store for us; in Your arms
we find comfort, at Your house we will wake.

12. More than anyone

I have been blessed so much in my life, so many people I
am grateful for,
By Your grace I received all, so many precious gifts for
me to adore.
Loving mother who bearing pain, nurtured me,
Protective father who sacrificed to fulfil my every need,
Wonderful sister who would make my smile wide,
Supportive brother who would stick by my side,
Invaluable friends to share my burden and pain,
Treasured teachers sharing knowledge for me to gain.
All of them are a gift from You; for each of them I thank
You being on my knees,
How great thou art! Through our lives, may Your glory
always increase.
Yet they are mortals, humans with limitations;
They are also weak like me, prone to fall for temptations.
But You still would stand by my side, being my shield,
Before anyone of this world, to you I will yield.
Mother may forget her love, father may lose his strength,
Sister would get tired, brother's love would fail to travel

any length;
Friends would end up betraying, teachers wouldn't live
up to their own lesson,
But You would not abandon me, no matter how bad gets
the season.
Your covenant was sealed in ultimate love for Your
creation, Your people save by the blood of thee;
Nothing can separate us from Your love, You are more
than anyone else for me.

13. Kindly take care

This world have lost its purity, it is turning more and
more bad,
The people You created in Your image are losing the
reflection of that image.
The worldly pleasures are deceiving us, we may look
happy, but deep down all are sad,
We pretend to live freely, but are actually trapped in evil
bondage.

We are drifting away from You, getting distracted from
what this world claims to offer,
In our folly, we are adding on to our blunders, increasing
the weight of our guilt.
The evil tricks us to chase all the wealth of this world,
trying to put all pleasures in a coffer,
We are trying to build our hope at the places You said
our faith shouldn't be built.

Look at us with compassion, consider our lack of
knowledge and forgive,

Prevent us from falling deeper into this abyss, kindly
take care.
Open our eyes, so we can see how the rest of our lives
should we live,
Give us the wisdom to discern and avoid the enemy's
snare.

The love from you that we receive is so great, nothing in
this world can compare,
How great thou art Almighty! You deliver justice and
still remain merciful.
We are so foolish that we're prone to stumble, but Lord
kindly take care,
Embrace us in Your love that we may never go astray but
always remain faithful.

14. My Worth

The day You created me with Your hands, I was the most
precious being;
You blessed me with life and allowed me to experience
all the gifts I've seen.
You have the authority over all lives, yet presented us
with a gift of free will,
Though You knew may fail, we may fall and stray away;
You loved us still.
Despite of being the sovereign King, You didn't keep us
enslaved,
All You asked from us was faith, to have in our hearts
Your name engraved.
But we rejected the wisdom You gave, thinking that
something better can we gain,
We were too sure we will thrive, but being away from
You only brought us pain.
In our folly, we still fail to surrender; we still try to run
away from You,
Thinking that the world can fulfil us, somewhere we
know that isn't true.

I was the most precious being only because You created
me,
Being away from, there's no worth in me which I can
see.
I am just a speck of dust, it's only from You I receive my
value,
How great thou art! I'll sing praises to You; for my worth
is all from You.

15. Do it again

You were always there with the ones who called You,
Blessed all those who had faith filled in their heart.
We call to the Lord who can win the entire battle with an
army of just a few,
It is not our strength, but Your grace; Oh Lord how great
thou art!

Parted the sea so that Your children would be saved,
Made the man who couldn't speak to free Your people
who were enslaved.
Anointed the one who was grazing his sheep; just a little
shepherd boy,
Strengthened him to use only a sling and stone against a
giant to destroy.

Let a giant fish swallow the man whole for his
disobedience,
Only to take him alive to preach the people about
repentance.
Called a man to walk on water towards You, as he would

walk on land,
Seeing the mighty waves, he stumbled but didn't drown
because You held his hand.

The man was on the bed, couldn't get up on his own,
You asked him to take his mat home, witnessing this,
everyone was left mind blown.
In Your presence, the lame would walk and the blind got
the sight,
Even the one filled with darkness, would surrender to
You and fill their hearts with light.

You had the authority over the fierce storms and the
ferocious waves,
Even the dead came back to life when You called them
out of their caves.
You were the only one with the authority to punish,
Still You chose to forgive and caused the sinners' sins to
vanish.

Would You do it again for me? I'm trapped in my sins, let
me be free!
I saw the might of the waves, I got scared by the storms
and I'm stumbling,
Could You hold my hands, be at my side; at the sight of
You, my enemy will flee.
Please do it again Lord, let Your hands protect me and

prevent me from crumbling.

How great thou art Almighty! No disaster can harm me
if You are there by my side,
I have disappointed You, sinned against You; I regret it,
I'm sorry.
Embrace me with Your forgiveness, receive me back
again as Your child,
If You are there to heal and nurture me, I will have
nothing to worry.

16. Sufficient

Chased the world in search of fulfilment,
Thought the world can satisfy,
Alas...How wrong was I!
Everything this world can offer is always insufficient.

Could money provide happiness? Can power make me
feel of any worth?
Or is everything a temporary; will time take it all away?
Will these help me to see tomorrow; if after this night
would I see another day?
Was I born to just enjoy these, was it all the purpose of
my birth?

Can I believe any human to stay? Wouldn't they always
find someone better than me?
Why should the betrayals surprise me; isn't that the cost
of trust?
Could anyone have pure love in their heart or is it all
adulterated with lust?
Forget about the world, am I good enough for others; can

in myself any value I see?

Oh no...nothing can satisfy or fulfil, no one can stay even
if they wish,
Riches will be lost, power will be stripped off and lust
will make one feel hollow,
I chased after the things with no value and the One I
should've looked upto, I failed to follow;
Stupid to think all these things would last, but in reality
everything would eventually perish.

But You are not of this world, Your glory has no limits or
boundary,
How great thou art! Only You could have pure love for
all,
Those who trust in You may stumble in this world, but
can never fall;
Because You only can fulfil, You are sufficient and only
You are worthy.

17. Peace

Amidst all the chaos of this world,
With these storms surrounding me,
I look for You my God,
For I know being with You, destruction, I will not see.

My own thoughts are haunting,
How can I escape myself, the brain of my own?
I look towards You, for Your help is my wanting,
To uproot the plants of this world, to destroy the seeds
evil has sown.

I wish to love others, but I still fail and judge,
Seeing myself as a sinner I later regret,
You would choose to forgive me, without holding any
grudge,
Teach me also to love like You, to forgive and forget.

In this world, what we experience is only numbness,
Only You can bless us with the real peace,

How great thou art! I will praise You for Your greatness,
With Your grace, all the chaos within me would cease.

18. May Your glory increase

Every word that I speak, every actions that I commit,
All pleasures that my eyes seek, everything to You I submit.
Each breath that I have left in me, without feeling any shame,
I wish to glorify thee, to forever praise Your name.
Through my life and the way I live, You I wish to please,
Nothing worthy to You can I give but I pray that through my life, may Your glory increase.
Only You are worthy to receive glory, Only You can handle it,
Without Your will, we wouldn't be having our story; we are here because of Your wit.
You are the almighty King, let only praise pour from my heart,
Songs about Your goodness shall I sing, Oh King, how great thou art!
Nothing to this world do I owe but for Your blessings I'll be forever grateful,
To You only I bow, keep me from evil, to You only I wish

to be faithful.
You have blessed me more than I deserve, such great is
Your love,
Let in Your glory my life preserve; with hopeful eyes, I'll
look up to You above.

19. Transform me

With love, You formed me as a reflection of Your own
image,
In this evil world's distraction, to that reflection I caused
too much of damage.
Still You loved me, suffered for my sake and offered me
salvation,
With Your healing touch, mend me again in Your image;
I wait for the divine transformation.

You have taught the value of forgiveness; unless I forgive
others, my sins would still remain,
The love You showed me, with other I have to share it,
that love I need to maintain.
Transform me so that such pure forgiveness and love can
be generated in my heart,
Let Your light reflect through my life, let others also
experience Your grace and say, How great thou art.

I was created with a purpose, I was supposed to be Your
child,

In Your love, You offered me to make a choice and in my
folly, I let the evil be my guide.
But You didn't hate me, You allowed temptations and
trials to teach me,
That all glory from this world would eventually fade and
fail; that only in You, my true worth can I see.

No amount of praise can suffice for Your glory, nothing
can we offer worth Your greatness,
For You wait for me to return back to You, eager to
embrace me; such great is Your kindness.
We were blessed with the grace we weren't worthy of ;
You withheld the punishment we deserved,
Transform me to be like You, enable me to serve instead
of having the desire to be served.

20. When I sleep

Since the moment You let me breathe, You have decided
my last day,
I don't have any command over life, but to the one
having authority I have this to say;
Seeing this beautiful world for the last time, one day I
will sleep,
Perhaps if I was able to earn someone's genuine love; for
my farewell, a few extra tears they would weep.
Before You let my earthy eyes to close, I have this one
request, one prayer;
Make me Your vessel in which with this world a portion
of Your love, You would share.
I have no words to explain, no science and evidence to
prove,
But there is a strange and wonderful longing; towards
You I wish to move.
Before You ask me to give back Your breath, there's one
more desire of my heart,
Even after my time here on earth, allow me to praise
You; How great thou art!

When I sleep, let no one despair, let one be sorrowful
remembering me,
But as long as You have allowed me to walk on this land,
let through me Your light they see.

21. Thank You

For considering me to be Your creation,
For creating me a work of Your hands,
For the wonderful gift of life,
For assigning a purpose for me;
I thank You Lord for these blessings.
For giving a sinner like me endless opportunities,
For sustaining me through all the storms,
For the blessings of family and friends,
For the grace that never left me;
I thank You Lord for these mercies.
How great thou art Almighty!
Nothing can match Your greatness,
The most powerful King You are,
Still You chose to grant love, kindness and forgiveness;
I thank You Lord for being Yourself.